SEASON
OF
Purpose

LaShae Wallace

ISBN-10: 1530616646
ISBN-13: 978-1530616640

Bible references are taken *from The Holy Bible, New King
James* Version, Copyright © 1982 by Thomas Nelson, Inc.;
New Living Translation NLT Copyright©2015 Tyndale
House Publishers; and *Holy Bible*, New International
Version®, NIV® Copyright© 1973, 1978, 1984, 2011 by
Biblica,Inc.®. Used by permission.

Published by **LaShae Wallace**

For information on this book, please contact:
LaShae Wallace at lashaewallace23@gmail.com
www.lashaewallace.com

WrightStuf Consulting, LLC, Columbia, SC
www.wrightstuf.com

Printed in the United States of America

Dedication

I dedicate this book to my beloved Grandma Dorothy Manigault who passed away 3/20/2016 at the age of 73. I was her oldest grandchild and she lived her life for the Lord. She always prayed for us, "There's something about the name Jesus," as I did for her...I will miss her humble spirit and angelic presence. She always told me to give my worries to the Lord, and everything will be alright! I love you Grandma.

Acknowledgements

I thank God for Jesus! Even in times of struggle, I trust Him. Sometimes you have to be reminded LOVE kept Jesus on the cross, not nails. He prayed, "Father if you are willing, take this cup from me; yet not my will, but yours be done." - (Luke 22:42) If it had not been for Jesus' obedience, I wouldn't be able to produce everything He destined for me.

All Glory belongs to God

Special thanks to every member of my family who have been there for me always. They have shown me tremendous love and support. (Mom, Dad, Nandi, Weldon, Jr., Theron, and Ezekiel, I love you); my Aunt Wandy, who bought a journal for me 12/25/13 and told me to, "Keep writing and share your spirit of peace and love"; and my Camp Long family who has challenged me to live a purpose driven life and GROW.

Thank you Carlos G. for seeing something in me that I didn't see in myself, and hiring me to make a difference in many at-risk female teenage lives. I love your heart. Your prayers, support, and encouragement mean the world to me. Little did I know the impact I would make and accepting my calling to Counseling. Sis Beverly, for taking me under your wings, and being a great spiritual mentor and hair stylist! I'm so glad God placed you in my life. Pastor Travis Greene and Dr. Jackie Greene, thank you for your words of wisdom and praying for me when I partnered with Forward

City Church in 2017. God is intentional! I can't go without saying thanks to my best friend, Terrell McCutcheon, who I have dated since September 28, 2017 for sharing special moments with me through life and not only praying for me, but with me...for this is my *Season of Purpose*. Update: For it is God's plan that on May 10, 2019 I graduated from South Carolina State University with my Master's in Counselor Education and started my career as a middle school counselor. I love my AJMS family. God has brought me a mighty long way by Grace through Faith. My story; His Glory!

"Season of Purpose"

Sometimes it takes a painful experience to make us change our ways...

-Proverbs 20:30

Table of Contents

Introduction

A Time for Everything

Your future is BRIGHT because God is already there...I don't know what tomorrow holds, but I know WHO holds tomorrow

I realize "Closure becomes easier once you start to understand that was just a chapter of your life, not the whole story..." Be with those who make you laugh. Love without holding back. Don't wait to count the blessings in your life, but experience them every day! *Season of Purpose* is similar to my first published book, *Look At God*, which was filled with journal entries, Christian lessons, scriptures, and my journey striving to be the woman God called me to be. I started writing to encourage others at 17. I definitely have grown A LOT, especially spiritually.

I believe your life has purpose. Your story/testimony is important. Your dreams count. Your voice matters. You were born to make an impact. I've learned that my greatest test is being able to bless someone else while I am going through my own storm. It's crazy to me why my biggest disappointments end up birthing my biggest praise! My pain is truly preparation for my destiny! God is not punishing you, He's preparing you. Trust His plan, not your pain. I know the best is yet to come...God knows the right time!

(Time does not move God, but God moves time)

Time is your most precious gift because you only have a set amount of it. You can make more money, but you can't make more time. When you give someone your time, you are giving them a portion of your life that you'll never get back. Your time is your life. That is why the greatest gift you can give someone is your time.

It is not enough to just say relationships are important; we must prove it by investing time in them. Words alone are worthless. "Our love should not be just words and talk; it must be true love, which shows itself in action." Relationships take time and effort, and the best way to spell love is "T-I-M-E."...like my Grandma Wallace always says, "Love isn't what it says but what it does"

To wait upon the Lord builds character, perseverance, patience. The Lord's timing is His secret. His revelation is our testimony. The Lord may respond to a need in 10 minutes, 10 hours, 10 weeks, 10 years...and when it is manifested, it is beyond our expectations!

God has a purpose for my life far greater than my pain. I want to encourage you to not let the struggle you're currently going through keep you from the blessings that God has for you. Sometimes it takes a painful experience to make us change our ways...remember that.

God Bless

"God will make a way for you today. How do I know? Because He made a way for you yesterday..."

Chapter 1

Planting Seeds

I've learned that feelings come and go...grow spiritually! It doesn't matter how great you plant the crop if God never sends the rain and sunshine. Sometimes when you're in a dark place you think you've been buried, but actually you've been planted. When God wants you to grow, He makes you uncomfortable. Sometimes God redeems your story by surrounding you with people who need to hear your past, so it doesn't become their future.<= Those are a few quotes that have pulled me through.

I've grown tremendously since *Look At God*. I realize the devil had a plot, but God has a plan. "You intended to harm me, but GOD intended it for good to accomplish what is now being done, the saving of many lives."-Genesis 50:20. God has a perfect plan for us. He never does it all at once, just step by step because He wants to teach us to *walk by faith, not by sight.* Everyone isn't meant to be your friend or to stay in your life. God brings certain ones to you so you can plant a seed in their hearts, to witness, or a test. These are seasonal people. Don't worry yourself to why you lost contact or wonder why they disappeared. Your time was finished and His plan went forth. You might not understand the WHY but Trust Him. The enemy always fights the hardest when God has His greatest work in your future. TRUST THE PROCESS & keep on going through. Don't give up! Quitting is not an option in my life and it shouldn't be in yours either. God is leading you to a place of victory and peace...if you believe.

B.E.L.I.E.V.E

Because.**E**mmanuel.**L**ives.**I**.Expect.**V**ictory.**E**verytime

I believe God is the Joy and the Strength of my life

God is a healer

Keeper of my Soul

Sinner's Advocate

Restorer/Redeemer

Sustainer

Provider

Deliverer

Refuge

Light/Salvation

God will never change, but He can change your situation

God will make a way for you today. How do I know? Because He made a way for you yesterday, you're still here, still standing, still holding on. God never changes. He remains faithful even when we are unfaithful.

"Jesus Christ is the same yesterday and today and forever."- Hebrews 13:8

Sometimes God Doesn't Change Your Situation Because He's Trying To Change Your Heart.

Sometimes you have to encourage yourself. Jesus promised He'll take care of me. I want to inspire you to not *judge each day by the harvest you reap, but by the seeds you plant"* (Robert Louis Stevenson).

When I think of planting seeds, the word "Stewardship" comes to mind.

Stewardship defined is the activity or job of protecting and being responsible for something.

As a Christian it is important to understand, "The earth is the LORD's, and everything in it, the world, and all who live in it." –Psalm 24

We are to respond to our abilities (Be Responsible) for the gifts God has blessed us with.

The bible also says to, 'Teach us to number our days, that we may gain a heart of wisdom." –Psalm 90:12

My brothers and sisters in Christ never tire of doing what is good...God will give you favor for your failure "Stand firm. Let nothing move you. Always give yourselves fully to the work of the Lord, because you know that your labor in the Lord is not in vain."- 1 Corinthians 15:58

Now is the time to stir up the gift of God which is in you. I always remind myself I am blessed to BE a blessing.

Everybody can't do everything, but everyone can do something...

Win souls for Jesus = Christian experience

At the age of 24, I am reminded to not let anyone look down on me because I am young, but set an example for the believers in speech, in conduct, in love, in faith and in purity. −1 Timothy 4:12

We are to not only plant seeds for tomorrow and be a good steward, but tithing is vitally important. It's testing and proving God to open the floodgates of heaven and pour out blessings until we overflow...I don't know about you but I pray God FILLS ME UP until I overflow!

1 Corinthians 16:2 says, "On the first day of every week, each one of you should set aside a sum of money in keeping with your income, saving it up, so that when I come no collections will have to be made.

AND

If we trust God by tithing 10% (Matthew 23:23) His Word will not return unto him void and He says in Malachi 3:10, "Bring the whole tithe into the storehouse, that there may be food in my house. Test me in this," says the LORD Almighty, "and see if I will not throw open the floodgates of heaven and pour out so much blessing that there will not be room enough to store it.

God loves a cheerful giver. (2 Corinthians 9:7)

And I'll always remember the words the Lord Jesus himself said: 'It is more blessed to give than to receive. (Acts 20:35)

Give and it will be given to you. A good measure, pressed down, shaken together and running over, will be poured into your lap. For with the measure you use, it will be measured to you." (Luke 6:38)

We all know the saying in Spider-Man, "With great power comes great responsibility" & God says "to whom much is given, much will be required" –Luke 12:48 if we are blessed with talents, wealth and knowledge...it is expected that we use those well to Glorify God and benefit others. That is the main reason I'm writing this book...because When I stand before God at the end of my life, I would hope that I would not have a single bit of talent left, and could say, 'I used everything you gave me'. – Erma Bombeck

Chapter 2

Prayer Changes Things

There is nothing more powerful than praying God's own Word.

P.R.A.Y.E.R = Prayer Releases All Your External Resources

P.U.S.H = Pray Until Something Happens

P.R.A.Y= Praise Repent Ask Yes

God hears what is not spoken and understands what is not explained, for His love does not work in the lips or mind, but in the heart.

Our prayers always include our wishes and desires. There's nothing wrong with our wishes and desires, but prayers also have to include not my will but Thy will be done. – Kirk Franklin

Romans 8:26, "In the same way, the Spirit helps us in our weakness. We do not know what we ought to pray for, but the Spirit himself intercedes for us through wordless groans."

Our **prayers have** no **expiration date**. You never know **when** or **where** or **how God** will answer.

"If you only pray when you are in trouble, you are in trouble."

"Dear God, please:
Teach me.
Keep me.
Hold me.
Help me.
I want to be better
than I was yesterday." ♡

God has a reason for allowing things to happen. We may never understand His wisdom, but we simply have to trust His will.

His Will is always better.

After Job had prayed for his friends, the LORD restored his fortunes and gave him twice as much as he had before. – Job 42:10

If you believe, you will receive, whatever you ask for in prayer. – Matthew 21:22

Begin to live as though your prayers are already answered...🙏

Sometimes the greatest prayer is just saying, "Thank You"

or sometimes the best prayer can be as simple as saying, "God, please help"

We experience a lot of unnecessary frustration simply because we try to do things without God's help...if we aren't spiritually fed, how can we be spiritually led?

The devil's biggest lie is making us believe "it won't get better"

How does one grow? Study the Word of God, PRAY, and surround yourself with believers.

Wait on the Lord; His timing is perfect.

"Don't let yesterday's seemingly unanswered prayers stop you from praying in faith today." — George Muller

"One song can change a moment, one idea can change a world, one step can start a journey, but a prayer can change the impossible."

Always pray to have,

1. Eyes to see the best in people

2. A heart that forgives the worst

3. A soul that never loses faith in God

The nicest place to be is in someone's thoughts! The safest place to be is in someone's prayers! And the best place to be is in God's Hands! ... Humble yourselves, therefore, under God's mighty hand, that he may lift you up in due time. Cast all your anxiety on him because he cares for you.

1 Peter 5:6-7

6/22/14

Dear God, You have brought me to the beginning of a new day. I ask you to renew my heart with your strength and purpose. Forgive my errors of yesterday and help me to walk closer in your way today. Shine through me so that every person I meet may feel your presence in my soul. Take my hand for I cannot make it by myself. In Jesus name, I love you Amen.

7/24/14

Dear Lord, please help us to trust You and Your timing. Sometimes we tend to get impatient and we tend to take matters in our own hands. I know this is a weakness that most of your children struggle with. Let the Holy Spirit transform this part of our lives. Help us to trust You Lord and trust that Your timing is best, for

You have a perfect sense of timing. In Jesus name, Amen.

"You may not understand today or tomorrow, but eventually God will reveal why you went through everything you did."

7/30/14

Dear God, Thank you for the harvest that's coming. It might be today, it might be tomorrow. It might be next week, next month, or next year. Just at the right time I'll experience my breakthrough. Let me not grow weary or faint. Strengthen me to hold on and not give up while I stand on Your promises. You are a God who is faithful and true to Your promises. I declare that I'll keep pressing. I'll keep believing, and I'll continue to do what is good because my harvest of blessing it's on the way and so is yours. In Jesus name, Amen.

8/21/14

Hallelujah! Thank you Jesus! The wait was over...I graduated from East Tennessee State University May 2014 and walked across the stage the semester before with a Bachelor's of Science degree. I received a call from the director (Carlos G.) at the camp I wanted to work at mentoring at-risk females from the Department of Juvenile Justice after about 8 months of seeking employment. I knew this is where God wanted me to be. My heart was filled with praise. My cup truly overflowed. I couldn't wait to pour into the teenage females lives. Lord willing, everything worked together for my good. I've learned a lot in the process. Perseverance. Faith. Endurance. Courage. Ambition

9/8/14

Thank you, God, for the gift of life and life more abundantly —John 10:10 I can't help but praise You for ALL you've done. I'm blessed beyond measure. I pray Your glory reigns in me to these girls. I'm here to make a difference and know this is where you called me to be.

3/22/15

Dear Heavenly Father, sometimes you have to encourage yourself...I thank you for another day. Thank You Jesus for giving me a humble heart. This prayer is not only for me but for anyone reading this; May you bless me right now and fill me with your incredible peace. Wrap me in your love. May I feel confident and worthy. I pray I would grow closer to you every day. Fuel a desire deep within me to seek after you. I pray that I would lead a life by the example Christ set. May I face everything with courage and may

I walk in integrity. Help me with anything I'm struggling with, surround me with encouragement and give me your precious wisdom. May I experience JOY today. In Jesus name, I pray. Amen.

5/1/15

Dear Heavenly Father, Thank You for another day. My eyes haven't seen my ears haven't heard, my mind hasn't conceived what you have planned for me. My desire is to please you and do your Holy Will. Sometimes we don't see the hand of God in a situation until we take our hands off the situation...I'm praying for growth in every aspect of my life. I'm praying for better! Help me to be the woman you called me to be.

"It Pushed Me"

This is my testimony: God used everything I went through to make me who I am today and I'm grateful. "God gave me a vision of where I would be, but He didn't show me what I'd go through on the journey...but everything that I faced prepared me for what God has for me to do. So now that I'm here I can praise Him for all that I had to go through. What the devil meant for evil, God used to get the Glory! It pushed me into my destiny God used it to make me who He called me to be." — JJ Hairston and Youthful Praise

#THAT

I thank God for going through "that" Because of "that" I see beauty for what it really is. I see it not of its splendor only, but for the victory of its struggle. Because of "that", I see pain as an opportunity to grow. I see break ups and breakdowns as doors for breakthroughs. Most of all, because of "that" I see myself beautifully imperfect, but looking forward to getting it right. So to me "that" was all worth it.

— Landon Taylor

"Be joyful always, pray without ceasing, give thanks in all circumstances, for this is the will of God for you in Christ Jesus"— 1 Thessalonians 5:16-18

Pray not only because you need something but because you have a lot to be thankful for

The things you take for granted someone else is praying for

If at times you are tempted to be unhappy and sour, remember that somewhere on this very planet people are struggling and praying to God to bless them with something you already possess.

I want to encourage you to KEEP ON PRAYING!

Pray! God knows His perfect timing. He may answer right after you pray. He may wait weeks, months or even years. He will wait until He is most glorified in your situation...so don't give up. You can wait on the Lord and trust His timing. Keep on praying

(Luke 18:1, Psalm 77:11-14)

Prayer may not change all things for you, but it sure changes you for all things.

Chapter 3

Now Faith

Faith is your response to the promises of God for your life

Through it all, I've learned to trust in Jesus!

Never be afraid to trust an unknown future to a known God.

Doubt sees the obstacles. Faith sees the way.

Doubt sees the darkest night. Faith sees the day.

Doubt dreads to take a step. Faith soars high.

Doubt questions, "Who believes?" Faith answers, "I"

"For I know the plans I have for you," declares the LORD, "plans to prosper you and not to harm you, plans to give you a hope and a future. Then you will call on me and come and pray to me, and I will listen to you. You will seek me and find me when you seek me with all your heart. –Jeremiah 29:11-13

When a train goes through a tunnel and it gets dark, you don't throw away the ticket and jump off. You sit there and trust the engineer. Trust God no matter how dark your situation

My future is as bright as my faith and smile.

I love God; Serve Others

Gratitude is the highest expression of Faith

My hope is built on nothing less than Jesus blood and righteousness

On Christ the solid rock I stand, all other ground is sinking sand.

I've learned not to put my hope in man and false expectations. Totally depend on God and His will!

Knowing FAITH is the root of all healing is the greatest understanding a soul can have.

Your faith is the root; obedience is the fruit

God is eagerly waiting for the chance to answer your prayers and fulfill your dreams, just as He always has...but He can't if you don't pray, and he can't if you don't dream. In short, He can't if you don't *believe*.

"Now faith is confidence in what we hope for and assurance about what we do not see." –Hebrews 11:1

"And without faith it is impossible to please God, because anyone who comes to him must believe that he exists and that he rewards those who earnestly seek him." – Hebrews 11:6

In every situation, God gave me blessed consolation but He told me that if I had not gone through the storm I wouldn't know what a little faith could do.

August 28, 1968 –Martin Luther King Jr. said in his "I have a dream" speech

With this faith, we will be able to hew out of the mountain of despair a stone of hope. With this faith, we will be able to transform the jangling discords of our nation into a beautiful symphony of brotherhood. With this faith, we will be able to work together, to pray together, to struggle together, to go to jail together, to stand up for freedom together, knowing that we will be free one day.

I thank God for him and his vision.

Tilmon Keaton, author of Change your L.I.F.E, said, "Your goals are attainable, but it requires commitment in the face of struggle, and it requires faith in the midst of adversity.

Consequently, faith comes from hearing the message, and the message is heard through the word about Christ. – Romans 10:17

Jesus has first place in my heart, and I want to show you —- I'm believing you for more. I have radical faith. I can't see it right now, but I'm standing on your Word/Promises.

1. Seek God first

2. Pray continually

3. Work diligently

4. Love unconditionally

5. Have FAITH always

Sometimes, you have to take a leap of faith first. **The trust part comes later…***When God leads you to the edge of the cliff, trust Him fully and let go. Only one of two things will happen: either He'll catch you when you fall, or He'll teach you how to fly!*

Chapter 4

Saved By Grace

As long as there is breath in your body, you have a second chance.

"Grace takes the punishment we deserve and mercy gives us blessings we don't deserve. Many of our mistakes are made while we are trying to do the right thing. But God's mercy sets us free to keep trying even though we often make mistakes. Salvation is a gift-it is not something we have to earn. All we have to do is open our hearts and minds to receive. Grace finds us where we are but it never leaves us where it found us. It takes us and makes us into what God wants us to be."

A beautiful day begins with a beautiful mindset. When you wake up, take a second to think about what a privilege it is to simply be alive and healthy. The moment you start acting like life is a blessing, I assure you that it will start to feel like one. Time spent living is time worth appreciating.

If you're breathing, God still has PURPOSE for you. As long as you have breath somebody needs what you have. Your gifts, your talents, your love, your smile 😊

"For it is by grace you have been saved, through faith --- and this is not from yourselves, it is the gift of God --- not by works, so that no one can boast. For we are God's handiwork, created in Christ Jesus to do

19

good works, which God prepared in advance for us to do." –Ephesians 3:8-10

We are all sinners, saved by Grace.

"Because of sin we're never as good as we know we should be. Because of GRACE we're never as jacked up as we could be." -Lecrae

I never thought I was worthy of Your Grace but You gave it to me anyway

"God made him who had no sin to be sin for us, so that in him we might become the righteousness of God." — 2 Corinthians 5:21

Thank You Jesus! Great is Your Mercy towards us. Your true worth has absolutely nothing to do with your bank account and everything to do with your character. To be rich is not what you have in your bank account, but what you have in your heart.

"Empty pockets never held anyone back. Only empty heads and empty hearts can do that" -Norman Vincent Peale

Successful people build each other up. They motivate, inspire, and push each other. Unsuccessful people just hate, blame and complain.

Psalm 46:5, "God is within her, she will not fall; God will help her at break of day."

Always remember, you have incredible worth not because of who you are but because of WHOSE you are.

"If you don't believe in miracles, perhaps you've forgotten you are one" 😊

Miracles start to happen when you give as much energy to your dreams as you do to your fears. Change your focus, and you will soon change your life!

I'm so glad God loved me even when I had no desire to follow Him...He gave His only son that you and I could call Him Father.

"I can't brag about my love for God because I fail Him daily, but I can brag about His love for me because it never fails." God IS love — 1 John 4:8

Nothing you confess could make me love you less! —God

If you try to justify your sin, then you'll never acknowledge your sin. If you don't acknowledge your sin, then you'll never repent of your sin. If you never repent of your sin, then you cannot be forgiven for your sin. If you are not forgiven for your sin, then you can I be cleansed of your sin. If you're not cleanse of your sin then you are still guilty of your sin. "The wages of sin is death..." Romans 6:23

Stop trying to JUSTIFY your SIN. Instead, confess your sin.... when you surrender to Christ, then YOU are JUSTIFIED. "Not guilty.

Today, confess your sins to God, put your trust in Jesus to save you, and you will pass from death to life. You have God's promise on it.

Take a moment to pray, "Dear God, today I turn away from all my sins and I put my trust in Jesus Christ alone as my Lord and Savior. Please forgive me, change my heart, and grant me your gift of everlasting life. In Jesus' name I pray. Amen"

The sincerity of your prayer will be evidenced by your obedience to God's will, so read His Word (the bible) daily and obey what you read. #LookAtGod

The more you fall in love with Jesus, the more you are going to be compelled to do what He tells you to do.

You'll never find a perfect person in this imperfect world. Connect with the person that God gives you confirmation about, the one who encourages you to be all that God has created you to be, the one that complements your life in a way that you NEVER want them to leave your presence.

If you don't have trust and communication within your relationship, it will never reach its full potential

that goes for a significant other, working relationship, and most importantly a relationship with Christ! Talk to God, give Him your heart, and trust in the plan He has for your life...even when we can't fully understand.
—Daniel "Dflo" Flores

Marriage isn't a race. Don't rush to the altar. Build friendship, trust, and love. I started graduate school when I met Terrell. God told me before dating him to let go of the life I pictured, so He could give me the life He planned.

Love is like a seesaw; it's made for two people. So, when you go down, there's someone to lift you up.

What I've learned Purity is the most attractive thing. Not only does it show honor and self-respect, but also shows the depth of your relationship with God.

"God doesn't show your heart to everybody. He only shows it to people He can trust with it.

Dear Relationship, let the love that we have for God, be stronger than the love that we have for each other. He will hold us together when this world tries to tear us apart. — Trent Shelton

When the relationship is ordained by God, You don't have to force it to work. Place your heart in the hands of God and He will place it in the right hands of the right man or woman who He believes deserve it. Being married won't heal you, and being single won't kill you. Waiting on God is never a waste of time.

"You made me believe that God sends people in our life for a purpose. He sent you in my life to heal my soul and to soothe my broken heart. Thank you for coming g in my life when I was lonely and shattered. Thank you for understanding me when no one was even willing to listen to me. Thank you for accepting me just for what I am and just the way I am. You loved me and supported me when I needed it the most. Thank you for making my life extraordinary and magical. I am irrevocably in love with your soul. You make me a believer."

Ladies: A beautiful exterior presentation may catch his eye, but it's a beautiful Christ-like spirit that will influence him to pursue, engage, and give you his last name. Know your worth!

Sometimes God closes doors even when we are walking in obedience. Not that you have done anything wrong, but because He has something better for you. He knows we won't move forward unless our circumstances force us to. #TrustHim.

Live in such a way that those who know you, but don't know God, will come to know God because they know you... #Unashamed.

"What God knows about me is more important than what others think about me."

Chapter 5

Be Humble

I ended "Look At God" with this particular scripture...James 4:10, "Humble yourselves before the Lord, and he will lift you up."

God will take you through a season of humility to refine your character for elevation. Whenever you come up and out don't forget what you went through to get there. — Candy West

It cost $0.00 to thank God for the simple things like being alive.

'The man who is willing to do more than what He's paid to do...will soon be getting paid way more for what he's doing." #PassionOverPay —Tyrese

What does the LORD require of you? To act justly and to love mercy and to walk humbly with your God. —Micah 6:8

I've always stood on this quote from the 40th President of the United States of America; Ronald Reagan said, "If we ever forget that we are One Nation Under God, then we will be a nation gone under."

The bible says, "If my people, who are called by my name, will humble themselves and pray and seek my face and turn from their wicked ways, then I will hear from heaven, and I will forgive their sin and will heal their land." – 2 Chronicles 7:14

"Lord, I'm available to you. My will I give to You, I'll do what You say do.

Use me Lord to show someone the way and enable me to say my storage is empty and I am available to You."- Melinda Watts

My only desire is to please You, God

"I want to go higher in You Lord; I want to go deeper in You in Lord

I know that my ways are not Your ways but in Your will is where I'll stay...mold me, make, fill me...Higher in You" –Kelontae Gavin

"I have hidden your Word in my heart that I might not sin against you."

— Psalm 119:11

What God knows about me is more important than what others think about me. People will always have an opinion about you, but live your life for the Lord, not people. (Colossians 3:23)

People will criticize you, get used to it. As a child of God, you should expect people to hate you for no reason. They hated Jesus. It's time to grow some tough skin and learn that your happiness doesn't come from someone else's approval. Happiness is an inside job.

Heavenly Father, help us to be sensitive to your spirit. We're realizing day-by-day this is a spiritual battle and we need to be connected to the source, You. The more we try to do things on our own the more stressful we become. The less we pray the more we are unaware of fruitless people and tricks of the enemy. Therefore, we humbly come to your throne and ask in Jesus' name to anoint us with your wisdom and discernment. Father, our hearts are heavy. Some of us are confused, hurting, tired and want to give up. But the Holy Spirit inside of us encourages us to keep going. O'Lord, your thoughts and ways are much higher than ours. Nowadays people camouflage who they say they are and who they portray themselves to be; however, You know the true motives of people's hearts. Sometimes it feels like you're our only true friend. Above all things Lord we need to stay connected to you. In Jesus' name, amen!

When I say..."I am a Christian"
I don't speak of this with pride.
I'm confessing that I stumble
And need someone to be my guide.

When I say..."I am a Christian"
I'm not trying to be strong.
I'm professing that I'm weak
And pray for strength to carry on.

When I say..."I am a Christian"

I'm not bragging of success.
I'm admitting I have failed
And cannot ever pay the debt.

When I say..."I am a Christian"
I'm not claiming to be perfect,
My flaws are all too visible,
But God believes I'm worth it.

When I say..."I am a Christian"
I still feel the sting of pain
I have my share of heartaches
Which is why I speak His name.

When I say..."I am a Christian"
I do not wish to judge.
I have no authority.
I only know I'm loved.

-Carol Wimmer
Chicken Noodle Soup for the Christian Family Soul

Chapter 6

Resist the Devil

"You are so valuable that Satan held you as ransom, knowing your Father was so rich. He asked of God, 'What would you give to see this man/ woman freed? Your father came through 42 generations armed with love & wrapped in flesh & said 'This is how much my child is worth--& He hung His head , stretched out His arms, & died."

James 4:7-8, "Submit yourselves, then, to God. Resist the devil, and he will flee from you. Come near to God and he will come near to you."

No matter how positive you may be, the devil will send negativity your way to see how positive you will stay...

Don't discount the devil...Satan can do everything you can do but live Holy.

Don't let the devil ride — because if you let him ride He'll surely want to drive.

If you feel like God isn't close to you, ask yourself this, 'who do you think walked away?'

Stop blaming the devil...could it be you holding your own self (blessings, destiny) by not confessing #Repentance — Pastor James L. Rowson

SPEAK LIFE!! Be positive when speaking! ... Negative thoughts seem to just come to us ... but change your mind set...focus on seeing the positive in every negative situation... it may seem as though there is nothing good there but there is always a lesson to be learned...or insight to be gained...this thinking brings peace and is felt in the heart...Peace doesn't mean no arguments...no battles...no noise or no conflict...it means to be in the midst of those things and still be calm in your heart..

The favor of God is on your life and the devil can't stop it! Walk with you head held high.

'Surround yourself with people who will call on the name of Jesus with you'

Be thankful for your problems, because as long as you keep the faith...God will use those things that you think are burdens as footstools to take you higher in life. Your burdens are simply the blessings that others are praying for.

Chapter 7

Patience

God's answer is not always yes or no; sometimes He says, "Not now!"

We must trust God even when His answer is "wait"

Patience is a virtue. The moon and the sun learned that long ago that, if each patiently waits its turn, they will both have their chance to shine.

Be patient. When it is your season, it is your season. When it is your time, it is your time. When God decides to bless you, then you will be blessed and quite frankly, there is nothing any other person can do to circumvent, interfere, or obstruct it. God's "Yes" will always overrule man's no.

Every single thing that has ever happened to you until right now was preparing you for a moment that was yet to come. Don't go back to less because you are too impatient to wait on God's best!

March 4th, 2014, I prayed for the job at Camp Long and was hired September 1, 2014. I said, whatever is in Your will that's what I want in my life. I asked God to enlarge my territory. I prayed for increase and He blessed me!

Keep praying, but BE THANKFUL that God's answers are wiser than your prayers!

Moving forward in life isn't about what's happening to you, it's about what's happening in you. Let patience have its perfect work in your life - so you can be thoroughly equipped for every good work!

I'm a firm believer in writing the vision down and making it plain... (Habakkuk 2:2) a few of my goals in 2014 that I wrote in the journal my aunt gave me was to get:

1. Job √

2. Degree √

3. Own place √

4. Better person/ growth/ spiritually/ physically √

5. Travel √

6. Sell Books #LookAtGod...who would have thought over 500+ copies of my first published book is out in the world and you are reading my second. √

7. Impact/Serve √

It's amazing all of my goals 3 years ago have been fulfilled...#SeasonOfPurpose

The struggle is real, but so is God.

"Your grind should always exceed your struggle" – Kyle Greene

Living for Jesus doesn't always mean that everything will be easy, perfect or that things will work out according to what you prayed--- but it does mean that He will be with you along your journey. – Heather Lindsey

Don't let the speed of your blessing mislead you into thinking it's not coming slow progress is better than no progress.

SO many reasons God could of gave up on me, but He was patient...He saw a future in me. He's not like man, He could've walked out on me. When I called on You, Jesus, you kept me!

"Do you mind if I testify...tell you of the goodness of my Lord. Share some of what He's done for me. How He's opened up so many doors. You may look at me from the outside and think I got here on my own...but there's no way that you could ever know how much GRACE & MERCY I've been shown. If you look into my eyes, you'll see life has tried to get the best of me. But I know the giver of life personally He's the reason I write. His name is Jesus and He loves me and I know this because He died for me and He rescued me there's NO GREATER LOVE in the world. There are so many things I want to tell you of how He made a way for me. If He hadn't loved me through the mistakes I've made I just don't know where I would be. He showed me so much favor and now I understand amazing Grace through all of the pain all of the shame I realize there is nothing that can take your place... You looked beyond my faults and God I'm so grateful." — Smokie Norful

NEVER GIVE UP; Never lose hope. Always have faith, it allows you to cope. Trying times will pass as they always do. Just have patience, your dreams will come true. So put on a smile, you will live through your pain. Know it will Pass, and strength you will gain.

Chapter 8

Promises of God

God doesn't ask us to: understand, comprehend, or figure it out. He just asks us to: *Pray, Seek, Trust, and Obey.* -Isaiah 55:8

Trust in His timing

Rely on His promises

Wait for His answers

Believe in His miracles

Rejoice in His goodness

Relax in His presence.

Whatever you have been praying to God for, keep praying. God breaks CHAINS...Not PROMISES! – Wayne Williams

THERE IS POWER IN THE NAME OF JESUS TO BREAK EVERY CHAIN!!! That is probably one of my favorite gospel songs...Glory to God Tasha Cobbs

The reason I love God is because He keeps His promises...I'm standing on the promises of God.

There are over 7,000 promises in Scripture. Find the ones that pertain to your situation and rest in them during your test.

For all the promises of God in Him are Yes, and Amen, to the glory of God through us. Have you thought about the fact that God has already said "yes" to His promises in your life? You don't have to beg God to be good to you. You don't have to plead with Him to help you. God wants to help you. He wants to pour out His abundant blessing on your life. Scripture says His promises are "yes and amen." Amen means "so be it." In other words, it's a done deal. All you have to do is make sure you are living up to your end of the bargain. See, God's love is unconditional, but we have to obey His commands in order to see His promises come to pass. For example, Malachi 3:10 says that we have to bring our tithe to Him in order to see the windows of heaven open. It says in Deuteronomy 5 that we are to honor our parents in order to live a long life. The good news is that when we surrender our hearts to Him, He empowers us to fulfill every one of His commands. He equips us for every good work because He wants to see us live a blessed life. That's why His promises are "yes" and "amen."

2 Peter 3:8-9, "But do not forget this one thing, dear friends: With the Lord a day is like a thousand years,

and a thousand years are like a day. The Lord is not slow in keeping his promise, as some understand slowness. Instead he is patient with you, not wanting anyone to perish, but everyone to come to repentance."

I don't always understand what God is doing, but I do hold on to His promises and know He will make a way.

Be strong and courageous. Do not be afraid or terrified because of them, for the LORD your God goes with you; he will never leave you nor forsake you." – Deuteronomy 31:6

Peter answered him, "We have left everything to follow you! What then will there be for us?" (Matthew 19:27) ... Jesus said to them, *"Truly I tell you, at the renewal of all things, when the Son of Man sits on his glorious throne, you who have followed me will also sit on twelve thrones, judging the twelve tribes of Israel. And everyone who has left houses or brothers or sisters or father or mother or wife or children or fields for my sake will receive a hundred times as much and will inherit eternal life. But many who are first will be last, and many who are last will be first.*

In all things give thanks because you know that "God is faithful." What you're going through is no surprise to God. Don't focus on your situation but make it your decision to focus on the promises.

God has a desire to use you...embrace the Promise not the counterfeit. I give myself away so You can use me Lord.

Psalm 138:8

I find it to be amazing how God gives a word for one person and so many others can relate to it.

Always remember the battle is not yours, it's the Lord's (2 Chronicles 20:15)

When you are on the Lord's side, you are never at a disadvantage.

1. Pray

Don't wait until the battle is over; Pray now! Just a little talk with Jesus will make everything alright

Cast all your anxiety on him because he cares for you. – 1 Peter 5:7

Live a life of prayer ☺

2. Trust the Promises of God

The reasons we don't win...might be because we don't trust God's promises.

If God said it, I believe it.

3. Praise

Praise is what I do

Blessed is the one
  who does not walk in step with the wicked
or stand in the way that sinners take
  or sit in the company of mockers,
² but whose delight is in the law of the LORD,
  and who meditates on his law day and night.
³ That person is like a tree planted by streams of
water,
  which yields its fruit in season
and whose leaf does not wither—
  whatever they do prospers. − Psalm 1:1-3

From the rising of the sun until the going down of the same, He's worthy; Jesus is worthy to be praised.

We cannot expect to receive the promises of God without first doing what He has asked us to do — bear fruit.

But seek first his kingdom and his righteousness, and all these things will be given to you as well. − Matthew 6:33

Falling in love with Jesus was the best thing I've ever done.

There is more Joy spending a few minutes with Jesus then spending a whole day with the world.

If you saw the size of the blessing coming, you would understand the magnitude of the battle you are fighting.

Prayer: May God give you a sense of what He is up to in your life. May you see glimpses of the breakthrough that is just up ahead. May you with all your heart believe that trusting Him over what your eyes see, is totally and completely worth it. May you shift your weight off of your logical reasoning and onto the weightiness of His powerful promises to you. You have help and resources that go far beyond anything you could ever need... Smile with Joy and walk by faith today. He has you 😊 Susie Larson.

One of my favorite scriptures is Isaiah 54:17; "God never said the weapons wouldn't form He just said they cannot prosper!" The devil knows the powerhouses we could be in Christ and he brings problems and circumstances to distract and discourage us. But Christ already won the victory on the cross, all we have to do is keep the faith and keep surrendering everything to God! Keep that in mind whenever you are going through something. The devil can try all he wants, but God has the victory before the battle starts! Claim the victory and believe! —Ayodele Owolabi (Sunday Best Season 7 Top 20).

God Bless.

"God gives us dreams a size too big so that we can grow in them."

Chapter 9

Praise Him in Advance

I can't help but to praise God from whom all blessings flow
"It's almost impossible to bless the Lord with your mouth close. His praise must continually be "in your mouth" not on your mind."— Hart Ramsey

Jesus loves to hear the sound of praise...He inhabits the praises of His people. Never allow the volume of your problems to turn down the volume of your praise!!

All of my help comes from the Lord, the Maker of heaven and earth. – Psalm 121:2

Look within and find God; Look ahead to see God; Look behind to Thank God.

3/27/14
Dear Heavenly Father, I didn't get the fellowship with Global Health Corps as you already know and I saw it coming. However, I still believe you will bless me with a good paying job. I'm letting your will be done in my life. I'm chasing after you and doing what pleases you. Guard my heart and mind. Help me Lord! I need you, I want to dwell in your presence. Thank you for my life and life more abundantly. Lord, show me my calling, open doors for me. I want to walk/live in my

purpose. I love encouraging others and I will continue to do what you say do. Yes, to Your will, Yes to Your way, Yes I will OBEY.

I love you Lord. Thanks again for blessing me and thanks for this day. In Jesus name, I pray Amen.
This was a prayer/praise in advance and 3 years later God answered this prayer in more ways than one. I wanted to have "Look At God" moments and I must say God never ceases to AMAZE me!

God gives us dreams a size too big so that we can grow in them.
Have those "It would take an act of God" type dreams. Dream SO big that when it happens you know it was God because you couldn't do it alone. 🙌 -Baylor Barbee
In my first book, I talked about how I was prayerfully going to graduate from college with a Bachelor of Science degree...well I did it and dedicated my degree to my parents, they never gave up on me even at my lowest points. They taught me the true meaning of this quote "Success is not final, failure is not fatal: it is the courage to continue that counts." One of my greatest accomplishments was graduating from college. The road was not easy but I wouldn't trade my experience for anything. #SCSU #ETSU #IDidThat...& if it's God's will I will continue my education. None of this would be possible without #Jesus #ThankYou 🙌😌

11/23/14 — My 23rd Birthday

I'll give you 3 reasons "God deserves our thanks." - Psalm 103:1-12. Psalm teaches us to praise and glorify God with thanksgiving...even in hard times, think of the goodness of the Lord. God says that when His people are thankful to Him. This is a form of worship that moves the heart of God. Jesus is the source of my prosperity.

    1. Because of His forgiveness
God doesn't treat us as our sins deserve or repay us according to our iniquities. —Psalm 103:10

    2. Because He's a Healer
Jesus is on the mainline—- tell him what you want.

"Praise the Lord, my soul; all my inmost being, praise his holy name." —Psalm 103:1

    3. Because He satisfies our desires with good things
God is Good ALL the time

I've learned not to let circumstances silence your praise...find a way to THANK GOD during your struggles, because it's all in His plans to take you higher.

A.C.T.S = Adoration. Confession. Thanksgiving. Supplication

Now unto him that is able to do exceeding abundantly above all that we ask or think, according to the power that worketh in us. – Ephesians 3:20

I've seen too many victories to let defeat have the last word.

I opened up my heart to Jesus…I talked to Him and asked for His guidance. Just one word made a difference.

Chapter 10

God is...

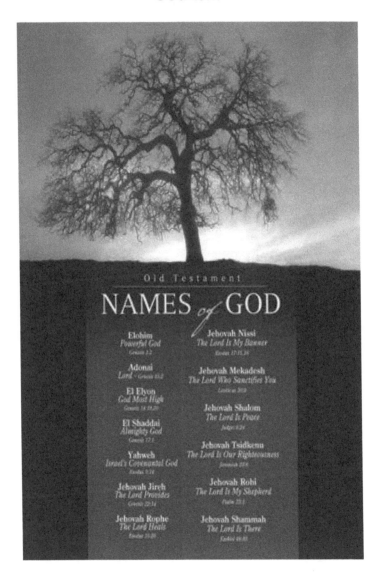

As you do not know, the path of the wind, or how the body is formed in a mother's womb, so you cannot understand the work of God, the Maker of all things.
 – Ecclesiastes 11:5

God is still working for you even when the odds are working against you. If God is the beginning and the end, why do we worry about what we are going through when we already have the victory?!

In 2015, I got my second tattoo it says "Enough". I am enough. Even if I feel like I'm lacking, I am fearfully and wonderfully made. When I feel the need to strain

and strive or when I feel guilt from thinking I didn't do enough...I remember that I am only human and I give the best I can in the moment...and that is indeed enough. Regardless of the situations I face, I believe The Lord Is able to see me through...He is doing a work within me...His grace is sufficient. He is more than enough for me. (2 Corinthians 12:9)

I can give you 12 reasons why God is good:

49

1. January

2. February

3. March

4. April

5. May

6. June

7. July

8. August

9. September

10. October

11. November

12. December

AND

7 reasons why He is great:

Sunday, Monday, Tuesday, Wednesday, Thursday, Friday, and Saturday He kept me.

God is ABLE

He is able to heal you

He is able to keep you

He is able to protect you

He is able to make your enemies your footstool

He is able to help that ministry grow

He is able to provide for you spiritually and naturally and meet every single need.

He is able to save your loved ones and convert them into true believers

He is able to mend your broken heart

He is able to give you more wisdom, more knowledge, more power, more strength

Don't place limits on what our Lord can do because all things are possible with Him

— Positivity Inspires

One of my favorite verses in the Bible, one that assures me that there is nothing or no one that can compare to what God is: "What then shall we say to these things? If God is for us, who can be against us?" (Romans 8:31) Almighty God is sovereign over all things and He is untouchable. Nothing can match His

Glory, strength, power, might, knowledge, forgiveness, blessings, riches, love, mercy, grace, omnipotence, omniscience, omnipresence, skill, handiwork, greatness, holiness, righteousness, availability, sensitivity, patience, tenderness, peace, graciousness, gentleness, self-control, joy, kindness, faithfulness, goodness, strategic ways, agape love, bravery, consistency, intentionality, humbleness, willingness, sympathy, empathy, beauty, authority, and anything else you can possibly think of. HE IS AWESOME!

At my lowest: GOD is my HOPE.
At my darkest: GOD is my LIGHT.
At my weakest: GOD is my STRENGTH.
At my saddest: GOD is my COMFORTER.

Let the world know that God is the anchor of your soul!
God is my strength. Strength like no other. Reaches to me. In the fullness of His Grace. In the POWER of His name. He lifts me up! — William Murphy

John 12:32, "And I, when I am lifted up from the earth, will draw all people to myself."

There is no place you can go that God will not be there. There is no struggle so great that God can't help you. When you've lost all hope, cry out to God as Jonah did. God will hear you.

Too many people focus on the wrath of God but not enough focus on the Love of God. Maybe if we start telling people how much God loves them, they can allow themselves to be loved out of any situation instead of scared out of it.

"God is Love" -1 John 4:8; 1 John 4:16

My life and My whole eternity belong to God. All this stuff is temporary. Money, fame, success...temporary. Even life is temporary. Jesus that's eternal. —Willie Robertson

Chapter 11

Greater is Coming

"The greatest glory in living lies not in never falling, but in rising every time we fall" –Confucius

When you depend on God everything works for your good.

"Greater will never come if you never learn to be content and happy *with* and *where* you are."- Pastor Chris Holloway

How do you expect your greater to come, if you aren't bearing any fruit?

What are you doing to help someone?

Your greater is in your *fruitfulness* and *faithfulness*

I've learned that sometimes God closes a chapter or a door for your protection. He loves you that much to not allow you to suffer more than you are able to bear. Accept it as the will of God...and KNOW He has something greater coming your way!

"Pay attention to your struggle. It's trying to show you something about you necessary for this next phase of your life. I know you're ready to get out of your situation, but understand, there's some stuff that you can learn only in the midst of the struggle. Pay attention, the struggle is happening for you, not to you."

— My Brother Ryan Sebastian Carson

Everything you're going through is just preparing you for everything that God has called you to be. Don't let the struggle take your faith, let it strengthen it.

Also keep in mind that the struggles that you face in life are meant to make you better, don't let them sour your attitude or mindset, and make sure that you continue to try with every morsel of fight left inside of you. Strive for becoming the best you, not becoming the perfect you, because when you reach for perfection you reach for something that can only be attained by reversing the hands of time.

Don't let the pain from what you've been through overpower God's influence of where He's trying to take you. He wants to heal your heart, then send you out to share His name, while helping others get through their situations.

God chose you to be an agent of change. Always push and encourage those around you to do better, be better and live better! [100]

The secret to being more is not associating with less
-Mr. Brent

At the end of the day, it's not about what you have or even what you've accomplished. It's about what you've done with those accomplishments. It's about who you've lifted up, who you've made better. It's about what you've given back.

God wants us to live like the grass. Even if it's stepped on, crushed, burned and cut; it always persists and grows back even greener and stronger.

I believe that one of our greatest opportunities to change the world starts by investing in the life of a child. That is why I'm so passionate about serving the youth, they are our future! So you never know who you touch. You never know how or when you'll have an impact, or how important your example can be to someone else

"Do you know that nothing you do in this life will ever matter, unless it is about loving God and loving the people he has made? -Francis Chan

Ask yourself this question, *Are we in love with God or just His stuff?*

One of my favorite gospel artists, Brian Courtney Wilson, said it best in his song "Worth fighting for"

"...Now I'm moving by faith and not by sight towards victory by the power of Your might. You're straightening out my past and opening every door. I am Your child and I'm worth fighting for.

Eyes haven't seen. Ears haven't heard (1 Corinthians 2:9) all You have planned for me and nothing can separate me from Your love (Romans

8:39) when there's so much more still worth fighting for.

I'm pressing towards the mark because the calling on my life is worth fighting for...I'll keep my mind stayed on You Jesus because the Peace it brings is worth fighting for...this world is not my home but Your kingdom here is worth fighting for...I have a mansion over in Glory and my new home is worth fighting for. Hallelujah! My Praise is worth fighting for..." *Worth Fighting For* - Brian Courtney Wilson

Because Jesus thought I was WORTH saving gives me every reason to give Him All the Glory, Honor and Praise and tell everyone I know...He cleaned me up inside, kept me and thought I was die for so He sacrificed His life so I could be FREE, so I could be whole! – Inspired by Anthony Brown and Group Therapy

I realize there is no greater that is *greater* than God's Glory.

At the end of the day, I have to look at myself and say, "Did I glorify GOD today...in my actions; thoughts; deeds; words; and decisions?" You see, God created us for His glory. Anything that I have done; said or thought that DOES NOT glorify God, requires repentance ... #ExamineYourself

The bible says, "Everyone who is called by my name, whom I created for my glory, whom I formed and made" — Isaiah 43:7

'For in him we live and move and have our being.'As some of your own poets have said, 'We are his offspring.' -Acts 17:28

It's not about me; it's about Him! #GloryBeToGod

When Solomon finished praying, fire came down from heaven and consumed the burnt offering and the sacrifices, and the glory of the LORD filled the temple. – 2 Chronicles 7:1

Therefore, we do not lose heart. Though outwardly we are wasting away, yet inwardly we are being renewed day by day. For our light and momentary troubles are achieving for us an eternal glory that far outweighs them all. So we fix our eyes not on what is seen, but on what is unseen, since what is seen is temporary, but what is unseen is eternal. – 2 Corinthians 4:16-18

God always has something for you, a key for every problem, a light for every shadow, a relief for every sorrow & a plan for every tomorrow. Accept all that is given to you with an open mind. Every gift, whether it warmed your spirit or brought you disappointment is a blessing. Learn from yesterday, live for today, plant seeds for tomorrow, live a life worth living. The philosophy of life is to make the most of it, enjoy the happy moments, and challenge the challenges thrown at you. Anyone can give up; it's the easiest thing in the world to do. But to hold it together when everyone else wouldn't understand if you fell apart, because of what has gone on in your life that's true STRENGTH. See life in a positive way through any kind of condition life may throw your way...

There is something about a person filled with HOPE. I must do my best to stay positive and to see the challenges that come in my life as opportunities to build character and prove my faith, then I know God will get me where I need to be, right on time.

Where there is life, there is hope. Jesus is not dead, He's alive. Whatever situation you may be facing today that seems hopeless or impossible, Jesus can resurrect it and bring it back to life. He is the same yesterday, today, and forever. The same Spirit that resurrected Jesus from the dead lives in me and you. Speak life over yourself and your circumstances and watch God work!

It's so easy to get discouraged and give up, but God wants us to be so full of hope that we just can't help but believe for the best.

Remember to always start your day with gratitude. Quite often we take our blessings for granted. We forget to appreciate the people or things we already have in our life and we strive for other things that we don't have in our life. But, by doing so, we don't enjoy the beautiful people or things we already have in our life. So, take a moment of your busy schedule every day to be thankful for the countless blessings that God has showered on each of us. You will notice that it will bring you so much peace when you know that you already have so much blessing in your life

"Delight yourself in the Lord and He will give you the desires of your heart" – Psalm 37:4

Conclusion

Purpose

Your life might not be perfect but that doesn't mean your life doesn't have PURPOSE. It takes a STRONG person to trust God's purpose without understanding the path. Sometimes your plans have to fail, so God's purpose for your life can prevail. There is a place of God's purpose, without a purpose, life has no meaning. Purpose gives us hope. His Will is what we ought to pursue. Without purpose, you make choices based on circumstances. Your life purpose is to use your own personal transformation to help transform society. Once mentored by another, you will now mentor others. If you don't enjoy doing what you're doing...you're not there. When you're living in your purpose, every day is a happy day. When you're living in your purpose there is a place of provision. Where God guides, He always provides.

When you're living in your purpose, there is a place of God's power. God wants to use our weaknesses for His Glory. Your purpose is defined in Him!

In life, you'll realize that there is a purpose for every person you meet. Some are there to test you, some will use you, some will teach you, and some will bring out the best in you. Each person comes into this world with a specific destiny — you have something to fulfill, some message has to be delivered, some work has to be completed. You are not here accidentally — you are here meaningfully. There is purpose behind you. God intends to do something through you.

I don't want God to take away a gift He gave you because of disobedience. Use the gifts God gave you to glorify Him and not please your sinful desires.

Obedience is better than sacrifice.

Seek God's presence, not his presents.

"One thing I ask from the LORD, this only do I seek: that I may dwell in the house of the LORD all the days of my life, to gaze on the beauty of the LORD and to seek him in his temple." — Psalm 27:4

God kept you for a purpose. Before you let go...Try God/ Trust God/ Tract God

God has a purpose and plan for each season of our lives. Be faithful, enjoy where God has you now, and know that before long you'll be experiencing a whole new season in your life.

Tamela Mann sung it best,

"Never knew my life could be this way...I never knew the sun could shine all day...Never thought I'd live beyond my past...until I found Jesus...I never thought I'd be in this place. Oh, I'm glad I'm living my life in this place. I just have to take a moment and say

Thank you Jesus for my life and life more abundantly! I praise You, I lift You up, and I magnify Your name.

I'm just a nobody trying to tell everybody about somebody who can save anybody #Jesus

"And we know that in all things God works for the good of those who love him, who have been called according to His purpose" -Romans 8:28

That's why my heart ♥ is filled with praise

If there is no passion in your life, then have you really lived? Find your passion, whatever it may be. Become it, and let it become you and you will find great things happen FOR you, TO you and because of you.

There comes a certain point in life where we discover that life isn't about us, but our footprint we leave behind on this earth.

Never look down on anybody unless you're helping him or her up, Because It's nice to be important, but it's more important to be nice.

When I'm helping people make sense of their lives, everything about my life makes sense to me. One day I woke up to a text message from my sister in Christ who said, "Good morning woke up this morning and thought of you! You're a very amazing person, very supportive of other people and an uplifter to your friends. Your praise and your smile encourage me! I'm so proud of you for your love, your intelligence, and memory of the word of God! You will go far in life! Keep on doing good things in life, continue to uplift others, pouring into people and God will open up the windows from heaven and pour you out a blessing you want even have room enough to receive! Thank you so much for being you! Love you and remember I still need your book -Phylicia

"With God ALL things are possible..." –Matthew 19:26

I hope this journey through my journal entries and personal experiences spoke life into your situation. Always remember it doesn't matter how many times you've read the bible front to back even this book filled with scriptures...if you don't have a relationship with Jesus, you just have information." – Tasha Cobbs

"For the Son of Man came to seek and to save the lost." -Luke 19:10

God is my passion, my creator, my God. I'll forever give Him Glory and Honor

I believe our prime purpose is to Praise God for ALL He has done. Worship Him, proclaim His greatness, and accomplish His Will. Our purpose in this life is to help others, and if you can't help them, at least don't hurt them.

My favorite Christian artist Lecrae said it best, "I know one thing's true:
> I don't even really deserve to know you
> But, I-I'm a witness that you did this, and I'm brand-new So, I-I'm read' to go, and I'mma tell the world what they need to know. A slave to myself, but you let me go, I tried getting high but it left me low You did what they could never do You cleaned up my soul and Gave me new life - I'm so brand new And that's all that matters
> I-I ain't love you first, but you first loved me
> In my heart, I cursed you, but you set me free
> I gave you no reason to give me new seasons, to give new life, new breathing
> But you hung there bleedin', and ya' died for my lies and my cheatin', my lust and my greed, (and Lord!)
> What is a man that you mindful of him?
> And what do I have to deserve this lovin'?

TELL THE WORLD

"For I am not ashamed of the gospel, because it is the power of God that brings salvation to everyone who believes: first to the Jew, then to the Gentile." — Romans 1:16

"How can I say that I love the Lord who I've never ever seen before?

And forget to say that I love the one who I walk beside
each and every day
How can I look upon your face and ignore God's love,
you I must embrace
You're my brother, you're my sister
And I love you with the love of the Lord" -Koinonia
(1 John 4:20)

"I love you with a perfect love and you have purpose."
— God

"I believe our prime purpose is to Praise God for ALL He has done. Worship Him, proclaim His greatness, and accomplish His Will."

Confirmations

Ms. LaShae I honestly can't thank you enough for supporting me through every obstacle I had to take to leave this program successfully. It's crazy on how close you can become to someone in what little time they have together. I've become so close to you in the past few months we've been together. It's going to be weird not seeing you on a day to day basis. Your words of wisdom have truly pushed me to be a better person each time those words came out of your mouth.

You helped me get back in touch with the Good Lord Almighty and I pray He blesses you with a long fulfilled life. You have such a huge heart, you would literally give the shirt off your back to help anyone in need. Anyone you come across will simply feel welcomed because of your kindness and warmth you fill the world with. You are such a special person, I know God isn't finished with you yet. You're so strong, I know you will accomplish any problem life throws at you.

So many others need someone in their life like you and I pray you continue to change lives like you changed mine. You've become such a huge impact in my life, I now thrive more in living a life with Jesus down the narrow road and encouraging others to do the same. Just like you encouraged me. It's true when they say the Lord works in mysterious ways and I thank him every day for mysteriously placing an amazing woman in my life. Thank you so so much for having faith in me when I lost what little faith I had in myself. Now it's time to take flight and put everything you taught me into work. You truly have encouraged me to help others and I appreciate you more than you realize. I love you!! GOD IS GOOD All the time. God Bless! ~Magan C.

****

Dear Ms. LaShae, one of my favorite FI's. I'm going to miss you dearly. You taught me a lot about the bible. You helped me understand the bible better. I believe in God and his word to the fullest but I've had my doubts and then there you were who made me not question him. You're a very sweet kind-hearted person. I know I could come to you and talk about anything. When I first got here it was something about you at first I didn't know what it was I got to know you and talked with you and it was that you loved and worshipped God. We could just sit and talk about God all day every day. I hate to leave you Ms. LaShae but my time has come FINALLY! I will never forget about you and I will definitely keep in touch. Also I'm ready for your next book. I love them! Keep writing! I love you Ms. LaShae. Stay Sweet! Love Always, ~Destini

****

Ms. LaShae I love your book it helps me learn a lot about life...it is so amazing how you can write about your life in a book and let the world see it. You are so confident in yourself and your book, and that is one of the things I love about your personality. Your book is the reason I want to get closer to God. ~Tamia

****

Ms. LaShae, First off I want to say thank you. You were always kind and patient with me. You are such a sweet person. You showed me that the whole world is not just full of hurtful and cruel individuals. You let me know that there are still some good people. Coming to Camp Long and meeting you, Ms. Andrea, and Mr. Chuck showed me that not everybody has given up on me. Y'all gave me hope and a reason to push forward and now I believe in myself. Thank you for being you and refusing to be otherwise. I'm glad I got the chance to meet you. Don't ever forget me! I love you! Sincerely, ~Lauren

****

LOOK AT GOD!!! Y'all don't Understand!!!
Last night I met this great Author of this Wonderful book...LaShae Wallace. This was not planned! In fact I met her a year ago but didn't know she was the Author of one of my most loved books!!

AS GOD WOULD HAVE IT...I VENTURED TO HER PARENTS HOUSE last night where she was visiting & staying for the night!!!!

LaShae's book....has been my daily bible & inspiration for months! I take it everywhere I go! I have it sitting on my desk and when people come to my office they say "Look At God." I smile....and we begin to give God Glory!!
LaShae,17yrs of age at the time, now 24, writes this book while in the LAND OF LONELINESS . She takes us through her life... using dairy entries & letters. She transfer her sounding board from FACE BOOK TO PAPER &PEN!

She shares her up and downs with us! Her battles with depression and her struggle with self-acceptance, LaShae evokes our attention by using Bible verses to show us how...GOD has EQUIPPED us.... in his Word... to deal with challenges, broken hearts disappoints, and self-esteem issues!! She tells us...you don't have to Go it ALONE! This book is for everyone especially our youth. ~Joy
****

Just wanted to let you know, that I think you're an awesome young woman with a heart for God. It is refreshing and inspiring to know that there are people in our generation still on fire for God. ~Iris

71

****

LaShae, just finished reading your book. Loved it. Loved the way you wrote it! I am encouraged to be a better Christian, and feel it is a light to the right path for anyone that doesn't know the Lord. I commend you for writing this book and look forward to your next. I know how proud your parents must be, I plan to share your gift with as many people as I can. God Bless! ~Cherrie C.

"Look At God" prepared me for my "Season of Purpose".

~ LaShae Wallace

Made in USA - North Chelmsford, MA
1033390_9781530616640
12.09.2019 1307